Creative Hand Embroidery

Exquisite countryside scenes in simple stitches

Wild orchids
Jean Mills
See page 1.

This unusual embroidery was inspired by a visit to a nature reserve near Northwich in Cheshire. As Jean explains, 'The soil from the construction of the M6 was tipped on to this land and after a few years wild orchids started to appear!' For the orchid petals, and for the curly grasses in the foreground, Jean has used silk which she stained with poster paints and then stiffened with PVA. Small lazy daisy stitches form the top of the flowers, and a variety of different sized and shaped fly stitches make up the rest of the grasses. The dragon-fly has transparent fabric wings and a stitched body which has been worked in tiny black and blue straight stitches.

Lace butterfly
Barbara Griffiths
See opposite.

In this embroidery, a stiff, transparent fabric has been used for the wings of the butterfly. Stained and stiffened silk has been gently folded to create the leaves, whilst the stems and flowers of the cow parsley have been worked in fly stitches and French knots.

Creative Hand Embroidery

Exquisite countryside scenes in simple stitches

SUE NEWHOUSE

SEARCH PRESS

First published in Great Britain 1993
Search Press Limited, Wellwood, North Farm Road, Tunbridge Wells,
Kent TN2 3DR

The author would like to thank her mother, Dorothy Howorth, her friend, Letty
Molloy, and her husband's secretary, Grace Burke, for helping to type and check
the manuscript; Hee-bee Designs of Willow Green, Cheshire, and Mrs G.M.
Parker of the Patchwork Gallery, Knutsford, Cheshire, for the loan of the equipment and materials illustrated on page 16; and, most particularly, all of her
students for allowing her to use their embroideries, without which the book
would not have been possible. Her sincere apologies are extended to all those
whose work has not been included due to lack of space.

ISBN 0 85532 727 8

If you have difficulty in obtaining any of the materials or equipment mentioned
in this book, then please write for further information to the Publishers, Search
Press Ltd., Wellwood, North Farm Road, Tunbridge Wells, Kent TN2 3DR

Mountaineer
Eva Meadowcroft
See opposite.

Eva created this scene for her son,
who is a climber in his spare time.
Her ability to paint helped her to
embroider the planes of colour on
the rocks, which she worked solely
in straight stitch. She used fly
stitches for the trees at the base of
the rocks, and a few French knots
for the foliage at the edge of the
water (which she had painted in
previously).

Printed in Spain by A. G. Elkar S. Coop, 48012 Bilbao

Contents

Introduction

In 1978, my two small sons became the children of a one-parent family. Like many people under stress, I needed a full-time, consuming interest. I embroidered a tree.

I still have that tree, one inch high in all its glory and looking for all the world like an autumnal lollipop, with buttonhole bars for the trunk and a few crude French knots on top. It was my first step. What would the same tree look like in other seasons? What would happen if I put it in a field, in a garden, against a wall, or beside another tree? Soon, the

Pergola and flower border
Marion Lewis

The idea for this embroidery came from a birthday card. The arch is made from real twigs, and scraps of mauve fabric form the clematis flowers which encircle it. The flowers in the borders consist predominantly of lazy daisy stitches and French knots, whilst the cliff and the path are made up of straight stitches. The daisies in the foreground have been worked on cold-water soluble fabric.

number of trees grew until I had a whole forest of them lying around on odd scraps of fabric. One day, a friend of mine said, '. . . very nice, but what are you going to do with them all?' Being more business-minded than me, she suggested that I should frame them and that she would sell them. We did just that.

My enjoyment in embroidering the countryside grew, and people began to ask where could they learn to do similar work. Hesitantly, I started my first class and, currently, I hold eight two-hour classes per week.

This book is for those of my students who would like twenty-four-hour classes, seven days a week, with no summer break. It was they who encouraged me to write it, and it is their embroideries, not mine, which fill its pages. I hope that, like my first tree, it will provide the first step for you. Everyone sees things in different ways, so there are no right or wrong ways of interpreting the countryside, just easier or more complex ways. My aim is to make it easier for you.

Boat on a lake
Anne Follows
Loaned by kind permission of Margaret Dawson.

This delightful scene proves that it is not essential to use masses of stitches in order to make a good embroidery. Using her knowledge of watercolour painting, Anne painted the silk background, fully intending to embroider all over the top of it. However, after a few French knots it became clear to her that not many more stitches were necessary. She worked the boat in straight stitches, added a small row of straight stitch grasses in the foreground, and finally attached a few fabric leaves on the left.

Just looking

**Monet's grain stacks: end
of summer**
Jill Milne

*This embroidery was inspired by a
visit to an exhibition of Claude
Monet's paintings at the Royal
Academy, and, in Jill's words,'The
work is an interpretation, in
stitches, of Monet's use of colour and
brush strokes.' It is made up of
masses of pink chiffon under and
over the stitches, and the large stack
in the foreground has been worked
on cold-water soluble fabric.*

Before putting needle to fabric, it is very important to allow yourself
time to get to know the subject that you are planning to embroider. A
friend of mine who is a builder once told me that when measuring and
cutting wood you should measure ten times and cut once. I believe that
this maxim applies equally to embroidery – look ten times and embroider only once. If you wish to create a countryside scene, then you must
have a knowledge of the ways in which different trees and plants grow,
not necessarily botanically but certainly visually. I have noticed that
those of my students who love their gardens and the countryside find
this subject easier to grasp than those who garden only through
necessity. This is because, without realizing it, the plant-lovers really

look at plants, not just at their colour, but at their shape, how they grow, and their relationships to other plants growing around them.

How observant are you? I am sure that as you begin to study your everyday surroundings you will be amazed at the richness of colour and texture to be found in the most common of plants and in the most mundane of places. For example, are you aware of all the wild flowers and varieties of grasses that grow at the sides of roads, in urban hedgerows, and on the central reservations of motorways? Even when the summer is over, these sites can look wonderful, particularly when the dead grasses are coated with a sprinkling of frost or a gossamer cobweb. Look, too, between paving stones, down drains, and at the bases of buildings where the wall meets the path – you are likely to discover all sorts of intriguing little plants sneaking amongst the bricks and stones.

Of course, gardens and parks are the obvious places in which to spend time looking at plants. In particular, they offer excellent opportunities for studying the way in which different plants relate to one another, in

Mountains in Nepal
Leila Sutcliffe

Leila was the first of my students to develop and use small silk flowers, a technique which she kindly explained to the rest of us. For this embroidery, she painted the mountains on a separate piece of silk, which she then appliquéd on to the silk background in front of the sky. To create a misty effect, she attached chiffon over the top of the mountains. Finally, she added the flowers and foliage in the foreground.

terms of colour, tone, and texture. For example, you may discover that a straight-leafed iris shows up well beside a wallflower, which in turn looks good beside a variegated nasturtium, which again looks different alongside an aubrietia crawling across the ground. Likewise, you may find an herbaceous border fascinating even though there are no flowers in sight, just a variety of greens and different shaped leaves.

In my opinion, some of the most interesting views of the countryside can be found at ground level. For example, try lying on your stomach in a field of wild flowers or uncut grass and looking through these to the distant landscape at the back of the field. If you do this in the morning with the sun behind you, then you will notice that the hedge and trees at the back of the field are quite colourful. If you go back to the same place in the evening with the sun shining into your face, then you will notice that there is less colour in the distance except for the sky, which could well be a blaze of colour.

Usually, the nearer a subject is to your eye, the larger, darker, and

Alpine meadow
Pamela Skelhorn

This scene was inspired by a picture postcard of meadow flowers. After wetting and staining the silk for the sky, Pamela trapped a small piece of fabric between the silk and the cotton sheeting to create the hill on the right-hand side. She used a mixture of fly stitches and French knots to suggest the trees on the horizon, and a mass of straight stitches for the meadow grasses. For the individual grasses and flowers in the middle distance, she worked seeding stitches, lazy daisy stitches, and fly stitches. Finally, she added texture to the foreground in the form of blanket stitch grass heads, tufted flowers, a variety of fabric leaves and flowers, and daisies which she worked on cold-water soluble fabric.

Lavender field, Norfolk
Mary Noden

*Colour, tone, and perspective have
been used to excellent effect in this
embroidery of a lavender field.
Firstly, Mary worked the buildings
in simple straight stitches and
covered them with chiffon to give a
misty morning feel. Then, she
spotted the field with paint,
planning to cover it with threads.
However, as the embroidery
progressed, it became obvious that
this was not necessary, and so
Mary limited herself to a mixture
of French knots and seeding
stitches, which she worked solidly
on the left-hand side and more
sparsely towards the right.*

more colourful it is. If you sit on the edge of the field, then you will be
able to see clearly the shape of the grass or flower immediately in front
of you. You can see the pollen and stamens, you can count the petals,
you can see whether the stem is smooth, angular, furry, straight, or with
stems branching off. If you then move a few hundred yards away, you
will get a different impression, as the flower or grass becomes part of a
mass – a blob of colour. You can no longer see each individual petal and
leaf. You may also become aware that your one poppy, for example, is
not alone and that fifty yards further into the field there are hundreds
of them, interspersed with the odd ox-eye daisy. Now, try looking
across the field to the tree at the back of it – the tree will look pale and
just a few inches high. Then, walk towards it. By the time that you have
reached the middle of the field it will appear darker and taller. Continue
across the field until you are only a few yards from the tree. It will now
be considerably taller than you and look a lot darker. Also, you will
notice that instead of a greyish pale green haze sprinkled over it, looking

like a million French knots, it now has a multitude of leaves which range in shades of green and look no longer like French knots but more like lazy daisy stitches.

Without realizing it, you are now beginning to learn about tone and perspective. Find a long brick wall with a door or a gate in it. Stand in the middle of the opening, facing up or down the wall, and then take a step to the left or the right. Now, look at the wall. The bricks immediately in front of you will appear to be considerably larger than the bricks one hundred yards further down the wall. Look, too, at the cement lines on the wall. The cement lines straight in front of your eyes will appear to run straight into the distance, whereas the cement lines holding the bricks together on the lower section of the wall will appear to angle up as they go into the distance. Look up at the cement lines above your head, and follow one to the end of the wall with your eye – it will appear to dip down.

Lupins
Ann Ford

This attractive scene, inspired by a picture in a book of gardens, reflects Ann's love of lupins. The two main flowers are made up of bullion knots which 'hang' inside inverted fly stitches, whilst the rest of the flowers and the foliage consist of a mixture of lazy daisy stitches, straight stitches, fly stitches, and rings of blanket stitches. Stained and stiffened fabric leaves make up the foreground, and a miniature fork adds further textural interest.

The Rickinghalls
Jean Mills

A visit to her daughter's home in the Suffolk village of Rickinghall inspired Jean to create this attractive scene. The stitches used include straight stitches for the buildings, roads and field, a mixture of fly stitches, crocheted chains and seeding stitches for the trees, fly stitches for the individual grasses in the field, seeding stitches and French knots for the small, yellow flowers, and lazy daisy stitches and French knots for the daisies. The boulders in the background are made from small pieces of stained silk, whilst the grasses in the immediate foreground consist of slivers of stained and stiffened fabric. The telegraph pole and painted village sign are made from tiny off-cuts of wood.

Given time and practice, these simple looking exercises will increase your visual knowledge of a wide variety of plants and landscapes, and give you the confidence that you need to begin embroidering your own garden or countryside scenes. I have found that after just one term most of my students are observing more of the world around them – even their holiday photographs start to consist of ground-level views of grasses and wild flowers, with just a hint of a view of the distant Himalayas, Alps, or Cairngorms! Of course, ideas can be gathered from many sources, and as well as your own photographs or sketches you can use magazines, holiday brochures, and gardening books to find inspiration. Remember, also, that you need not stick rigidly to an original picture but can use it simply as a starting point to alter as you wish.

Most scenes can be interpreted with a surprisingly small number of stitches, and in the next section you will find instructions for working all of the basic stitches used in this book.

Mary's garden
Edna Tait
Loaned by kind permission of
Mary Downes.

Edna embroidered this scene as a
present for her friend Mary. She
was particularly inspired to create
it by the eucalyptus tree, which
reminded her of her visits to
Northern Spain. The tree itself
has been worked on cold-water
soluble fabric, whilst the little
figure in the corner of the wall has
been stitched on silk and then
stretched over a piece of mounting
card before being appliquéd to the
background. The wall is made up
of stained silk and straight stitches,
with pieces of chiffon added to give
a shadowy effect. The bush on the
right consists of couched threads
and lazy daisy stitches, the path is
indicated by straight stitches, and
the real stones around the pond are
also secured by straight stitches.
The flowers and the foliage include
a mixture of lazy daisy stitches,
straight stitches, blanket stitches,
seeding stitches, and French knots.

Making a start

This section contains all of the information that you need in order to embroider a simple meadow scene. If you spend a little time mastering the basic techniques, then I am sure that you will soon develop the confidence and the skills necessary to create your own original designs.

Materials and equipment

When advising upon the selection of materials and equipment, I always try to recommend items that are simple, economical, and easy to obtain. However, there are no hard and fast rules, and I suggest that you treat the following list as a guide only. For example, if you would prefer to use fabric paints rather than poster paints, or starch rather than PVA stiffener, then do so. Likewise, there is no point in purchasing a size 9

A selection of materials and equipment required for creative hand embroidery: white habutai batik silk; stranded cotton embroidery threads; white cotton sheeting; embroidery ring frames; cold-water soluble fabric; poster paints; PVA adhesive; water; white modelling clay; pair of embroidery scissors; fine needles; pencil eraser for use on fabrics; air-soluble and water-soluble pens; 6mm (¼in) square paintbrush; white mixing palette.

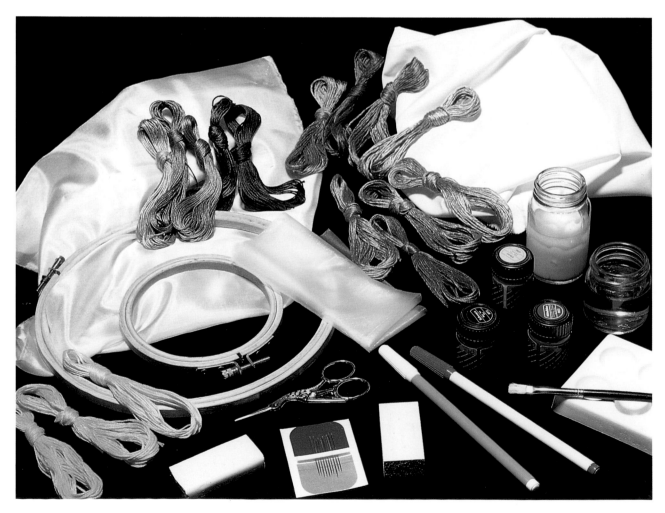

needle if your eyesight will not allow you to thread it, so, simply use the finest that you are able to cope with. Also, remember that you do not need all of the materials and equipment listed here in order to produce a good embroidery. Imagination – one of the most important elements in any good embroidery – is free!

Materials

Good quality white cotton sheeting

White habutai batik silk, or a similar finely woven white fabric

Cold-water soluble fabric

Stranded cotton/silk embroidery threads in a selection of carefully chosen colours

Black, yellow, and blue poster paints, and water

PVA roller-blind stiffener

PVA adhesive

Mounting card

White self-hardening or oven-bakable modelling clay

Florists' wire

Equipment

Two embroidery ring frames, one 7.5–10cm (3–4in) in diameter and one 20–22.5cm (8–9in) in diameter

The finest needle that you can thread, and a fine crochet hook

Small, sharp pair of scissors

White plate or palette upon which to mix paints

6mm (¼in) square paintbrush

Water-soluble or air-soluble pen

Pencil eraser for use on fabrics

Craft knife

Binding an embroidery ring frame

A ring frame consists of one wooden or plastic ring fitted inside another, between which the fabric is tensioned, the stretched fabric surface uppermost. In order to prevent the stretched fabric from slipping, it is a good idea to bind the inner ring with some white cotton sheeting. Simply tear a few lengths approximately 2.5cm (1in) wide, wind them around the ring, and secure the last one with a few stitches on the inside. When working on a very fine fabric, such as habutai batik silk, you may find that it is necessary to bind the outer ring as well.

An embroidery ring frame, the inner ring of which has been bound with strips of white cotton sheeting.

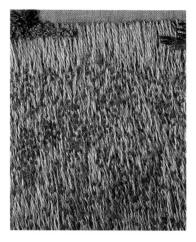

Straight stitches and red seeding stitches, from an embroidery by Leila Sutcliffe. (See page 61 for the complete scene.)

Stitches

The more skills that you learn, the more exciting your work will be, so before you embark upon your first embroidery I suggest that you spend some time practising the following basic stitches. Use one strand of embroidery thread only and the finest needle that you can manage. Also, even when practising, always stretch your fabric in an embroidery frame before starting to stitch, and check it frequently to ensure that it remains taut. I check mine every time that I rethread my needle.

Straight and seeding stitches

Straight stitch is the simplest and most flexible of embroidery stitches, consisting of a single line which can be worked in any direction. Straight stitches can be spaced widely apart or closely together, and can be uniform in length or of varying lengths. Each stitch is worked independently. Bring the thread up through the fabric in the required position for the first stitch. Take it down before coming up in the position for the next stitch.

Seeding consists of minute stitches of equal length, which are worked at random in all directions. Bring the thread up through one hole in the weave of the fabric and take it back down, if possible, in the next, making the 'seeds' appear as specks rather than short stitches.

straight stitch

seeding stitch

Yellow tufted flowers, from an embroidery by Pamela Skelhorn. (See page 11 for the complete scene.)

Tufting

Use at least six strands of embroidery thread for this easy method of tufting. Take the needle through to the back of the fabric, leaving about a 1.25cm (½in) length of thread on the front. Make a very small straight stitch on the back and bring the thread through to the front again. Cut all of the threads close to the fabric to make the tuft.

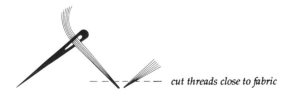

cut threads close to fabric

18

Blanket stitch

This stitch is worked from left to right. Bring the thread up through the fabric on the required baseline of the stitch. Insert the needle to the right of and above the thread, and bring it out directly below, on the baseline, with the thread under the needle. Pull the needle through to make a straight, upright stitch with a loop on the baseline. Continue making stitches as required, and finish by taking the thread through to the back of the fabric on the baseline and then securing it.

Rings of blanket stitches, by Anne Follows.

Lazy daisy stitch

This is also known as detached chain stitch. Bring the thread up through the fabric and hold it down and to one side with your left thumb. Make a loop towards the right. Insert the needle almost where the thread first emerged and make a straight stitch across the back, bringing the needle out a short distance away over the looped thread. Fasten the loop in place with a small straight stitch. Either secure the thread at the back for a single stitch or bring it back through to the front in the required position for the next stitch.

Lazy daisy stitches, from an embroidery by Marie Bell. (See page 53 for the complete scene.)

Fly stitch

This stitch can be used singly, arranged in patterns, or made into a line. The 'tail' can be lengthened, and the length and angle of the arms can also be varied. Bring the thread up through the fabric at the top left side of the required position of the stitch. Hold the thread down with your left thumb, and insert the needle on the same level but a little to the right of where the thread first emerged. Take a small stitch downwards and towards the left, with the thread below the needle. Pull the needle through and then take it through to the back of the fabric to make a small stitch in the centre. Either secure the thread for a single stitch or bring it back through to the front in the required position for the next stitch.

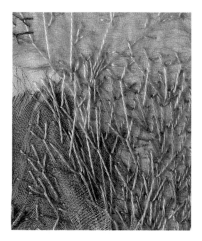

Fly stitches, from an embroidery by Renee Grundy. (See page 45 for the complete scene.)

French knots, from an embroidery by Gillian Nuttall. (See page 57 for the complete scene.)

Bullion knots, from an embroidery by Ann Ford. (See page 13 for the complete scene.)

Crocheted chains, from an embroidery by Renee Grundy. (See page 45 for the complete scene.)

French knot

Bring the thread up through the fabric in the required position and, holding it firmly with your left hand, twist the needle once around it. Still holding the thread firmly, next twist the needle back to the starting point and insert it close to where the thread first emerged. Pull the needle through to the back of the fabric, leaving a well-shaped knot on the surface. Either secure the thread for a single knot or bring it back through to the front in the required position for the next knot.

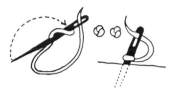

Bullion knot

Bring the thread up through the fabric at the left end of the required position of the knot. Insert the needle at the right end of the required length of the knot and bring the point out in the same spot as that at which the thread first emerged. Do not draw the needle through completely. Twist the thread around the needle as many times as needed to equal the length of the required knot. Hold your left thumb on the twisted thread, and draw the needle and thread through. Still holding the twisted thread, turn the needle back to where it was inserted and insert it again in the same place. Pull the thread through to the back of the fabric until the knot lies flat. Either secure the thread for a single knot or bring it back through to the front in the required position for the next knot.

Crocheted chain

Firstly, make a slip knot. Hold the crochet hook with the knot on it in your right hand, and slip the embroidery thread through the fingers of your left hand. Twist the hook under and then over the thread to make a loop. Draw the hook with the thread on it through the slip knot. Continue making stitches in this way until the chain is of the required length. Cut the thread and pull it through the last loop on the hook. Pull it tightly to close the loop and finish off the chain.

Interpreting the countryside with stitches

All of the stitches described on pages 18–20 can be used in a variety of ways to interpret many things. For example, fly stitches can be used to indicate trees, the heads of cow parsley, ears of corn, and many different grasses. French knots, if used in abundance, are ideal for representing trees on a distant skyline. They are also useful for creating the centre of flowers. Usually, just one knot is sufficient, but for flowers such as sunflowers a clump or mass is needed. Tufting is also very versatile. Tufts of variegated blue make wonderful cornflowers, whilst long and short tufts of variegated greens can be used to create chaotic clumps of grass.

Remember that a variety of different stitches can be used to represent one particular flower, depending upon its position in the landscape. For example, when creating poppies in the distance you could use red seeding – one stitch for one flower. In the middle distance you could use one red French knot, whilst in the foreground you could use four to five red French knots with one black French knot in the middle. If you require even more detail, then you could make a fabric poppy (see pages 40–2).

Bumble bees
Jenny Parker

In this delicate little embroidery, the bumble bees have tufted bodies and organza wings. The cow parsley consists of fly stitches, and its flowers are made from French knots with a pink seeding stitch in the centre of each. Soft shades of watercolour paint have been used to create the subtle background.

Stitching on cold-water soluble fabric

Cold-water soluble fabric is a colourless, plastic type of material upon which you can embroider all kinds of flowers and grasses. It is a wonderful invention, but it does require a little patience and practice if it is to be used successfully. The most important point to remember is that the more stitches you use the more secure the finished item will be. Here, I describe how to create a daisy. In fact, this is probably one of the most fiddly things to embroider because there are so few stitches involved in creating it. So, if you can master this, then you should have no fear of using cold-water soluble fabric in your embroideries.

First of all, put the inner ring of your small embroidery frame on to a table. Place the cold-water soluble fabric on top of it, and then place the outer ring on top of both and tighten the screw. Be careful not to stretch the fabric, as it will tear. To avoid this, some of my students prefer to use a double layer.

Next, bring your thread through to the front of the fabric, leaving at least a 1.25 cm (½ in) length loose on the back. Using lazy daisy stitch, start to embroider the petals, taking care not to pull the thread too tightly as you stitch. If you always stitch opposite petals, then your thread will keep passing back and forth across the middle of the daisy, helping to hold the flower together. Unless you are careful, it is very easy to end up with a ring of petals around a 1.25 cm (½ in) hole, which is not what is required! As you work, try to stitch over the loose thread at the back.

Rosebery Topping
Christine Flegg

This embroidery shows how cold-water soluble daisies can be used to enhance a quite simple landscape. Interest has been added to the skyline by allowing the flowers and the foliage to bounce up in front of the sky. The faint hill in the background (Rosebery Topping) has been made by trapping a piece of fabric between the silk and the cotton backing fabric.

Once you have completed all of the daisy petals, cut out the flower as closely as possible to the thread. Pierce it with a needle, so that the needle is holding it, then very carefully drip water on to it until the fabric has disappeared. You may find it easier to control the water if you use a small paintbrush. When you think that you have melted the cold-water soluble fabric completely, carefully slide the daisy off the needle and on to a non-absorbent surface to dry. Once it is dry, you will see that the cold-water soluble fabric has disappeared but has stiffened the thread. Any odd bits hanging from it can now be cut off without fear of the daisy falling apart. Also, if you notice that some of the fabric is still visible, then it is perfectly safe to repeat the process. The daisy is now ready to be stitched into place, using a large, yellow French knot through the middle.

As you become more adept at using cold-water soluble fabric, you may find it quicker to put all of the pieces to be dissolved into a sieve and run cold water through them. Also, a hair dryer can be used to help them to dry more quickly, but take care that they do not stick to the sieve.

Finally, if possible, do try to keep your remaining cold-water soluble fabric in a dry place. It is a good idea to buy only a small quantity at a time, as after a while it tends to become very brittle.

Sunflowers
Anne Parker

In this brightly coloured scene, Anne has used cold-water soluble fabric to create the large sunflowers in the immediate foreground. For those slightly further back, she has embroidered the lazy daisy stitches straight on to the background fabric. She has indicated the sunflowers in the middle distance with French knots, and those in the far distance with seeding stitches. The tree is worked in a mixture of fly stitches and lazy daisy stitches, with a blanket stitch bar for the main trunk. The fields in the distance consist of separate pieces of silk which have been painted and then appliquéd to the background, whilst a mass of French knots make up the horizon line.

23

Meadow embroidery

If you have never done any embroidery, then I advise you to try this simple meadow landscape before attempting to create your own scene. However, it is important to realize that the instructions which follow are really only a guide. There is no definitive way of creating a landscape, and if ten people were to do the same embroidery then each one would be slightly different. For example, some might feel it most important to concentrate on the horizon line, whilst others might prefer to keep the horizon line simple and concentrate instead on the foreground.

The main point to remember is to keep your first embroidery small, so that you are able to complete it quite easily. This will give you the confidence to embroider a slightly larger and more personal embroidery next time.

Materials and equipment

The materials and equipment that you need to make this embroidery are listed on page 17. The pieces of white cotton sheeting and habutai batik silk should both be approximately 25 x 25cm (10 x 10in) in size. Also, you will need the following colours in stranded embroidery thread: four muted shades of green (if possible, purchase shades with consecutive colour numbers), white, buttercup yellow, poppy red, pale pink, dark pink, blue, and black.

Method

1. Firstly, stretch the white silk on to your 20–22.5cm (8–9in) embroidery frame. To do this, take the frame apart and lay the silk over the inner ring. Then, press the outer ring over it. Pull the fabric out gently until it is taut, being careful to keep the grain straight, and tighten the screw.

2. Next, put a piece of white paper underneath the ring, lightly wet the silk with water, and gently brush a wash of pale blue poster paint across it, working from left to right with the grain of the fabric. The silk will start to sag when it is wet, so keep pulling it gently all the way around the frame, taking care to keep the grain perfectly straight. Dry the silk as quickly as you can, for example, using a hair dryer, so that the water does not leave any marks. Then, look critically at the blue colour. (The white paper beneath will ensure that you see the true colour.) Is it suitable for the sky? If you think that it looks too dark, then simply put it under a running tap. If it is too pale, then wet the silk again and add more blue. As a general rule, I advise you to err on the pale side – a sky that is too vivid does not usually look realistic. Once you are happy with it and it is completely dry, take the silk off the frame.

3. As it is so fine, the silk fabric needs to be strengthened before it can be stitched upon. To do this, simply back it with the white cotton sheeting, making sure that the grain of the fabric is running in the same

How to begin

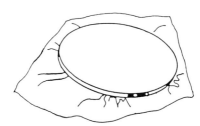

Stretching the silk on to the ring frame.

Meadow landscape
Sue Newhouse

Step-by-step instructions for embroidering this landscape are given on pages 24–30. However, if your finished embroidery does not look like this one then do not worry. Of the dozens that I see embroidered every year, no two meadows are exactly alike, simply because they have been embroidered by different individuals.

Embroidering the background

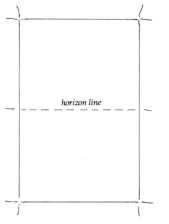

Marking the rectangle and horizon line with stitches.

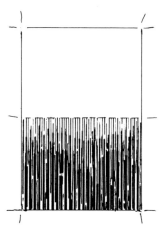

Embroidering the field, using straight stitches.

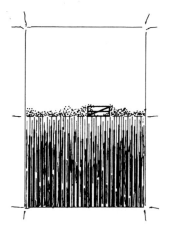

Embroidering the hedge and the gate on the horizon line, using French knots and straight stitches.

direction on both pieces. Then, treating them as one, restretch both fabrics on to the frame.

4. Mark in a rectangle, approximately 11.25 x 7.5 cm (4 ½ x 3in), with four large stitches – do not draw it in. Make sure that the grain of the fabric is running in the same direction as the longest sides of the rectangle. Then, approximately half-way up the rectangle, stitch a line straight across to mark the horizon line.

5. Thread your needle with one strand of the palest green thread (shade A) and, starting from the horizon line, work large straight stitches, ranging in length from 1.25 cm (½ in) to 2.5cm (1in), down the rectangle. Make sure that each stitch begins on the horizon line but ends at a slightly different level from the stitch before and the stitch after it. Keep the stitches close together and keep working back and forth until all the gaps have been filled. When no fabric shows through at all, the back of the field is complete.

6. For the middle of the field, thread your needle with one strand of the next, slightly darker, shade of green (shade B). Now, begin to blend in the new shade, again making sure that each stitch is of a different length from the one before and the one following it, and this time that the top line is as erratic as the bottom line. Overlap the row of shade A as much as possible, but keep this second layer of stitching lower than the horizon line. Continue working from left to right, or right to left, until this band of green has hidden the silk background and you have covered approximately two-thirds of the field.

7. Thread your needle with one strand of the next shade of green (shade C) and treat the third layer in exactly the same way as you did the second. Make sure that shade C slightly overlaps shade B and that all of the stitches are of a different length. If there are any gaps of silk showing through, then simply go back and fill them in until you have a completely solid field of grass, starting with pale green at the top and graduating to darker green at the base. If any of the overlapping shades of green are not blended together well, then thread your needle with one strand of the paler of the two shades and create a new band which overlaps both shades.

8. The next stage is to create an interesting horizon line by embroidering a hedge and a gate. Thread your needle with one strand of the palest green thread (shade A) and work two or three rows of French knots for the hedge. Work across the entire width of the horizon line, leaving a 1.25 cm (½ in) gap in which to embroider the gate, and try to make the top of the hedge as lacy as possible. Still using shade A, next create the gate posts by working two upright stitches, one on either side of the gap left for the gate. Using single straight stitches, stitch horizontally across the top, middle, and bottom of the gap. Then, work a stitch from the top

left corner of the gate across to the bottom right corner. Finally, to create an interesting shadow, sprinkle a few French knots at the base of the hedge, using green shade B.

9. If you wish, then you can also add a tree to the horizon line. Simply stitch it in with fly stitches, again using just one strand of green shade A. Use one large stitch for the main trunk and branches, and some smaller ones for the rest of the branches. Put in as many branches as you think are necessary, and make sure that you stagger them rather than joining them all to the main trunk at the same spot. Then, sprinkle small French knots in clusters all over the tree, using one strand of shade A. To finish off, add a few seeding stitches around the edges of the clusters.

10. Having embroidered an interesting skyline, the next stage is to create the impression of a million grass heads in the field, without actually having to embroider a million of them! In the middle one-third of the field, embroider about twenty grass heads, using the three shades of green that you have been using already. To signify a very basic seed head on a grass, firstly stitch one lazy daisy stitch. Immediately under it, cup it with a very small fly stitch. You can work one, two, or three of these stitches under each other, each cupping the one above. When you feel that you have made enough fly stitches, extend the centre stitch from the last one straight down to the base of your work, at a slight angle. This makes the stalk, and it will show up against all of the background stitches. Mix the shades of green so that the darker grasses show up against the pale green background and the pale green grasses show up against the dark green background. However, try not to put all of the dark colours at the top and all of the paler ones at the bottom, but scatter them as haphazardly as you can.

11. Now the field is ready for the flowers to be added. Here, I describe how to work six different varieties, but the number that you choose to include in your embroidery is up to you. You may decide that you wish to include all of them, or, alternatively, you may decide that you would prefer to create a field of poppies or daisies only. Whichever you choose, do remember that a round patch of flowers at your feet becomes an oval patch when viewed from a hundred yards. Viewed from a mile, it will be merely a line.

Daisies Thread your needle with a single strand of white thread and, working about 3.75 cm (1½in) from the base of the embroidery, make five, six, or seven very small lazy daisy stitch petals, all coming down from one central spot. Then, stitch a yellow French knot on the top of the spot where they all join. If you wish, then you can add a few stems and leaves to the daisy. Using one strand of your darkest shade of green (shade D), work five or six large fly stitches to create the stems, and add lots of little fly stitches down the stems for the leaves. Use a few single white French knots to indicate daisies in the middle distance, and a line

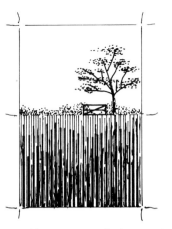

Adding a tree to the horizon line, using fly stitches, French knots, and seeding stitches.

Embroidering the details

Grasses (lazy daisy stitches and fly stitches).

Daisies (lazy daisy stitches and French knots).

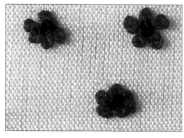

Poppies (French knots).

Buttercups (French knots, with fly stitch stems).

Cow parsley (French knots, with fly stitch stems).

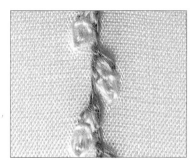

Foxgloves (lazy daisy stitches and fly stitches, with straight stitch stems).

of six or seven seeding stitches at the back of the field to indicate daisies in the distance.

Poppies These consist simply of five red French knots, worked very closely together, with one black French knot squeezed in the middle. As for the daisies, work the poppies about 3.75 cm (1½in) up from the base of the embroidery. Make one long stitch in green shade D for each of the stems, taking each stitch to the base of the embroidery. For a poppy bud, a small lazy daisy stitch, worked at an angle, will suffice. Cup the top of this stitch with an inverted fly stitch, making the centre stitch about 6mm (¼in) long . Then, to make the stem, take a long stitch from the end of this centre stitch straight down to the base. Use a group of red French knots to indicate poppies in the middle distance, and a line of red seeding for poppies in the background.

Buttercups For these, use single yellow French knots for the flowers and some long fly stitches for the stems. If you wish, then you can add green lazy daisy stitches to the joints of the stems to suggest leaves. Work an oval shape of yellow French knots to indicate buttercups in the middle distance, and a line of seeding for buttercups at the back of the field.

Cow parsley In order to add interest to the embroidery, this should be worked about twice the height of the daisies, poppies, and buttercups. Using either green shade C or green shade D, make large fly stitch stems and then almost, but not quite, a ring of smaller fly stitches on the top of each stem. Cover this pompon of smaller stitches with small white French knots. Complete the head by adding seeding stitches to any gaps around the edge.

Foxgloves Like the cow parsley, foxgloves need to be tall. To create a good effect, group two or three large ones together, with some French knots for the smaller ones in the middle distance, and a line of pink seeding for those disappearing into the far distance. If you look at foxgloves, then you will notice that some have flowers all the way around the stem, whilst others have them just down one side. Starting with the largest and nearest foxglove, firstly make the stem, using a long, green straight stitch. Then, thread your needle with one strand of pale pink thread and use seeding stitches to make the top one or two flowers. As you come down the stem, slightly increase the size of the stitches, and then, after making four or five, start to break into the smallest pink lazy daisy stitches that you can manage. If you wish, then you can cup each flower with an inverted fly stitch, in green, to indicate the calyx. As you work down the stem, increase the size of the lazy daisy stitches just a little. The choice is yours as to how many flowers you add to the stem. Now, on the bottom half of each of the flowers, superimpose two fly stitches, one the right way up and the other reversed to meet it. This creates the effect of a tube, which is essentially what an individual foxglove flower is.

Rosebay willowherb. Like foxgloves, these are tall and usually grow in groups. However, unlike foxglove flowers, rosebay willowherb flowers are made up of petals. Firstly, make three or four long green stems, using straight stitches. Then, choose a dark shade of pink thread and, starting at the top of the stem, make some very small straight stitches. As you work down the stem, gradually alter the angle of the stitches until they are coming out at right angles from the stem. Next, start to change the straight stitches into very small lazy daisy stitches. For the rest of the flowers, you can either continue using lazy daisy stitches, or you can use French knots. If you choose to use lazy daisy stitches, then start by grouping two together, then on the next flower down group three, and on the rest four. Try not to end up with a row of flowers down each side of the stem, but put one or two flowers in the middle of the main stem. Finally, in the centre of each flower, add one black and one white seeding stitch. For the leaves of the rosebay willowherb, use either green shade C or green shade D and add small fly stitches all the way down to the base of the stem.

Rosebay willowherb (straight stitches, lazy daisy stitches, French knots, and seeding stitches, with straight stitch stems).

12. The next step is perhaps the most difficult. To make your embroidery come alive, you need to add textures to both the flowers and the greenery. One way of doing this is to use cold-water soluble fabric. If you have never used this before, then I suggest that you spend a little time experimenting with it first (see pages 22–3). Carefully mount a piece of the fabric in your 7.5–10cm (3–4in) embroidery frame and embroider about ten grass heads, as small and as compact as you can manage them. Cut them out as closely as possible to the threads and then spear them on to a needle. Drip water all over them and place them on a non-absorbent surface to dry. With just one stitch for each, sew them on to the middle band of the field, ideally in an empty area. Three or four daisies made on cold-water soluble fabric will give a lift to your daisy clumps (see pages 22–3). Sew them into place in between your other daisies, using one yellow French knot for each. Now, stand back and look at your embroidery. Except for the bottom 2.5cm (1in), most of it should be pleasantly filled.

Adding textured flowers and grasses to the foreground.

13. If you lie down on your stomach in a field of wild flowers and grasses, then you will notice how many different varieties of leaves there are. Most of all, you will notice those within 5–10cm (2–4in) of you. It is these leaves and grasses that now have to be added to your embroidery. Firstly, you need to stain a small amount of your spare silk fabric green. To do this, mix a little yellow and black poster paint with plenty of water to make a murky colour which is a shade darker than the green threads that you have been using. Then, carefully brush the green paint on to the silk, making sure that you give the impression of stained, not painted, silk. Once the silk is dry, dampen it with a thin solution of PVA stiffener. This helps to stiffen the silk so that it will cut more easily, and it also helps to stop it from fraying. If the silk appears blotchy in colour then do not worry, as grasses and leaves come in all

Making a dandelion with tufted flowers and fabric leaves.

shades of green. Using a sharp pair of scissors, with blades about 5–7.5cm (2–3in) long, cut some long, fine blades of grass. Try to use a single cut, as a staggered one will produce a rather crooked blade. Cut a number of blades, in lengths varying from 1.25–3.75cm (½ –1 ½ in). As grass grows in clumps, you need to group your fabric grasses in clumps. For example, you might have a gap in your embroidery between the daisies and the poppies, so position the long grasses to fill this gap and come between, rather than cover, the flowers. Place groups of the shorter grasses under the daisies and poppies, making sure that all of the blades of grass are 'growing' from the base of your work. Attach each blade with a single stitch.

14. Another interesting way of texturing your embroidery is to add a few tufted flowers. To make a dandelion, firstly cut three or four petal-shaped leaves from a scrap of green stiffened fabric. Fold each leaf to make a 'seam' down its centre, and snip away small sections so that it looks rather like a small Christmas tree. For the flower, thread your needle with six strands of yellow thread and make a little tuft. It is not necessary to knot the tuft, as it is so small that it is unlikely to be accidentally pulled after you have trimmed it down to size. Cornflowers can be made in a similar way, using blue thread. Being taller than dandelions, they need to be positioned higher in the field, at approximately the same level as the poppies.

15. Finally, fill in any spaces that are left at the base of the field, for example, using a group of French knots or some individual strands of green thread which have been stiffened with PVA before being attached.

Variations on the meadow embroidery

Hopefully, by completing the meadow embroidery, you will have gained confidence in your ability to embroider a countryside scene and will now be ready to start creating your own original landscapes. For your second embroidery, I suggest that you try a simple variation on the meadow theme. This will give you the opportunity to practise, experiment with, and adapt the basic techniques that you have learnt already.

One simple, but effective, variation is to change the shape of your embroidery from a rectangle to a circle or an oval. Another is to increase the scale of your work slightly. However, I would not recommend that you attempt anything too large, unless you have plenty of time and patience! An area of the actual landscape which is quite easy to alter is the sky. For example, try using various tones of blue and adding a few clouds, either by brushing in hints of white or by lifting off some of the blue with a paper tissue. Think, too, about the skyline – why not add a distant house or church to it? You can do this quite easily by drawing the building on to the cotton backing fabric at the level of the horizon line, using a pencil or coloured crayon. Another alternative is to use a silhouette, that is, a piece of fabric trapped between the silk and the cotton backing. For example, if you wish to create a hill in the background, then simply cut out the shape in a fine fabric and place it between the silk and the cotton sheeting, making sure that the base of the silhouette touches the horizon line. Then, restretch the silk carefully so that the silhouette does not move. Whatever you choose to stitch on the horizon line will hold the silhouette in place. The foreground of the landscape also offers endless scope for variation. If you included a number of different coloured flowers in your first embroidery, then why not restrict yourself to just one type or colour in your second?

The embroideries in this section illustrate just a few of the ways in which the basic meadow theme can be developed. I am sure that you will discover others.

Thistles
Paula Hammond

Paula has used a wide variety of techniques and textures in order to make her embroidery as interesting as possible. If you look carefully, then you will spot seeding stitches, French knots, small bullion knots, fly stitches, tufting, and pieces of stiffened fabric. The fields in the background are made up of separate pieces of silk which Paula has stained and then attached in overlapping layers. Some of the grasses consist of a 1.25cm (½in) length of crocheted chain with a 5cm (2in) length of thread left for the stem, the whole of which has been stiffened with PVA.

Poppies and cornflowers
Audrey Thornley

This embroidery makes use of French knots and fly stitches for the trees, seeding stitches and French knots for the flowers in the far and middle distance, straight stitches for the grass, tufting for the cornflowers, and red stiffened fabric for the poppies. Layers of silk and chiffon have been used behind the trees to create an unusual skyline.

Bluebell walk
Barbara Griffiths

In this delightfully simple scene, Barbara has used just a mixture of straight stitches and French knots in blue and green, with threads of hessian twisted to form the tree trunks. She was inspired to create it by a photograph that she saw in a magazine.

Rosebay willowherb and heather
Louise Mulchrone

This scene consists predominantly of fly stitches, French knots, and straight stitches, with lazy daisy stitches used for the flowers of the rosebay willowherb. Unlike the sky, which was washed on to wet silk, the water was painted on to the silk when it was dry, using a reasonably dry brush, so that the colour would not run or bleed.

Rural scene
Norma Whittle

The idea for this landscape came from a greetings card. Like the embroidery above, the water was painted on to the silk when it was dry. The bulrushes consist of two rows of tufting each, and the trees have crocheted chain trunks. Other stitches include fly stitches, straight stitches, French knots, and seeding stitches. The rolling hills in the background are made from separate pieces of silk and chiffon which have been appliquéd on.

33

Wildlife garden, Chatsworth
Doreen Willows

This small, circular embroidery includes French knot and fly stitch trees, tufted mauve thistles, daisies which have been worked on cold-water soluble fabric, and stiffened fabric grasses and poppies.

Field of rape
Barbara Griffiths

This scene consists simply of a mass of seeding stitches and French knots, with green fly stitches in the foreground.

Poppies at Moseley Hall
Jennie Williams

Like the bluebell and the rape embroideries (see page 32 and above), this scene illustrates just how effective it can be to use only one type of flower in a landscape. To create her poppies, Jennie has used red and green stiffened fabrics for those in the foreground, French knots for those in the middle distance, and seeding stitches for the ones in the far distance. The poppy buds on the horizon line each consist of a red lazy daisy stitch cupped with a green fly stitch. The rest of the embroidery is made up simply of fly stitches, French knots, and straight stitches, with three small fly stitch birds in the sky.

The fisherman
Jacky Bennett

This appealing embroidery illustrates the fact that you do not need to use a wide variety of stitches in order to create an interesting scene. Jacky has simply used a range of different sized fly stitches, together with a few lazy daisy and straight stitches. To give the impression of water, she has painted the background silk (when dry, not wet as for staining the sky) and then covered it with a piece of chiffon. Also, to add further texture, she has included a number of fabric grasses in the foreground.

Stretching and mounting your embroidery

Once you have decided that you have completed your last French knot and you feel that your embroidery is well balanced, spend a few days looking at it critically. Are the colour and tone acceptable? Do you feel happy with the composition, and with the quality of your stitches? Once you have made the effort to frame your work, it is almost too late (although not quite) to start taking it apart or adding to it.

Take your embroidery out of the ring frame and cut off the excess fabric, leaving about 3.75 cm(1½in) of silk and sheeting around the embroidery. Then, cut a piece of mounting card approximately 3.75cm (1 ½ in) larger than this, and place the embroidery in the middle of it.

Now comes the difficult task of stretching. Almost everyone that I know recommends lacing the back, but I have found that it is extremely difficult to get the silk to stretch properly, so I am afraid that I recommend using PVA adhesive. Taking care not to move your embroidery from the middle of the mounting card, fold back the sky about 1.25 cm (½ in) and weight it so that it does not bounce back. Apply a thin line of PVA to the card, then let the cotton sheeting down so that it falls straight on to the glue. This stays wet for a few minutes, so you do have a chance to straighten the fabric and make sure that it is not cockled or warped. When this has dried, turn the board around and do the same to the bottom 1.25 cm (½ in) of the embroidery. This time, make sure that you keep the cotton stretched whilst the glue is drying, by dragging the sheeting down evenly with your nails. Then, glue down the sides, one at a time, making sure not to pull one side further over than the other, otherwise the embroidery will end up looking warped. As long as you made sure that throughout your stitching you checked the tension of your fabric and that it was straight, the silk should now fall relatively flat. Also, you will notice that the glue is about 2.5cm (1in) away from the embroidery – try your best to keep it that way and not let it run or creep any nearer. Once it is on your embroidery you will not be able to get it off, and although it will not be too noticeable to begin with, after a few years it will turn yellow.

Now, turn your embroidery again so that you can glue the sky end down first. Put a line of glue on top of the glue that is holding down the sheeting and, with your finger nails, gently drag the silk towards the edge of the mounting card. Keep stretching from left to right until the silk is glued down. At this stage, it will have ripples in it, running up from the stitches into the sky. Do not worry. Simply turn your embroidery around and glue down the bottom of it. Then, glue the two sides, one at a time, making sure that you glue and stretch evenly. The glue should still be a little damp, so look at the sky. If there are any bubbles in it, then using your nail on top of the glued bit, not below it, drag the silk out just a little more towards the edge of the mounting card. Keep doing this until the bubbles disappear.

Your embroidery is now ready to mount and frame, and I recommend that you do not try to economize on this. Having put a lot of work into it, surely it is worth mounting and framing well. Generally, I use a double mount, as this prevents the embroidery from being squashed against the glass. Of course, if your embroidery is very three-dimensional, then you will have to use an even larger number of mounts. Alternatively, you can add an insertion, either between the glass and the mount, or between the mount and the embroidery, in order to lift the glass from the embroidery.

Moving on

As you are probably beginning to discover, the more that you are prepared to experiment, the more interesting your embroidery becomes. However, if you wish to progress further still, then it is necessary to learn new skills. In this section, I describe a variety of techniques which will help to add a more three-dimensional aspect to your work.

Using appliquéd fabrics

An interesting three-dimensional effect can be achieved by appliquéing an extra piece of fabric on to your background silk and then stitching over it. For example, in the two embroideries illustrated here, carefully folded white satin has been used to create the impression of snow. In a similar way, it is possible to incorporate fabric animals into a countryside scene. Always remember to appliqué your shape to the background first. Then, if it does not work, you can start again easily without having wasted any time embroidering the rest of the landscape.

Winter sunset
Ewa Stratford

In this delicate winter scene, Ewa has made clever use of overlapping pieces of satin and a minimum of stitches. She has folded the satin in the foreground carefully to create an undulating effect, and has added small pieces of chiffon for extra texture. The only stitches she has used are fly stitches, seeding stitches, and French knots, with crocheted chains for the tree trunks.

Snow scene in a wood
Gillian Nuttall

The foreground of this embroidery consists of a large piece of carefully folded satin with areas of undergrowth which have been worked on cold-water soluble fabric. A few seeding stitches on the satin, and a clump of French knots immediately behind it, add further textural interest. The trees are made up of crocheted chain trunks and fly stitch branches and twigs. To achieve the subtle colouring of the background, Gillian firstly wet the silk and washed the colours across it. Then, she turned the frame through fifty degrees and stood it up so that the colours ran down and blended into each other.

Using stiffened fabrics

Stiffened fabric can be used to wonderful effect in a landscape, to create detailed, three-dimensional flowers and grasses. In the meadow embroidery, I show how to stiffen silk to make grasses and leaves (see pages 29–30). Here, I describe something a little more complicated – how to make an arum lily.

Firstly, stiffen a piece of white silk with a thin solution of PVA stiffener. Then, cut a small circle from it and roll this on to the top of a piece of florists' wire. Using one strand of dark green thread, bind the base of the rolled, white fabric on to the top of the wire, and then continue binding down the wire as far as you think is necessary to make the stem. Use the end of the thread to stitch the flower into place. For the lily leaf, paint some silk a mottled green colour, using a mixture of black and

Arum lilies, from an embroidery by Maureen Clunie.

The complete scene.

yellow poster paints. Dry the silk, stiffen it, and then cut out the shape of the leaf. Next, secure a piece of wire to the underside of the leaf with a few stitches. Use the remaining thread to bind down the wire and stitch it into place on the embroidery. By bending the wire carefully, you can either give the leaf a gentle curve or make it turn at a right angle.

The other fabric flowers, illustrated here and overleaf, are made in a similar way. Why not try experimenting with some ideas of your own? Depending upon the degree to which you dilute the PVA stiffener, you can either stiffen the silk just enough to stop it fraying, or so much that it looks and feels like plastic.

Water-lilies
Jean Mills

This embroidery contains the minimum of stitches. The lily pads are simply pieces of silk which have been painted and stiffened, as are the pink flowers. The goldfish is made from a piece of orange fabric which has been trapped between the silk and the cotton backing fabric, whilst the stems of the lilies are indicated by a few straight stitches also semi hidden beneath the silk.

Poppies
Joan Ollier

Joan's ability to make silk flowers helped her to create this unusual embroidery. The poppy seed heads are made from pads of green fabric bound with thread to the top of a piece of wire. A ring of blanket stitches creates the pattern on the top of each head, whilst the petals and leaves consist of stained and stiffened pieces of silk. The 'twists' of the love-in-a-mist are threads which have been dipped into a dilute solution of PVA stiffener, twisted, and then dried on a crochet hook.

Making and using miniature objects

An unusual way of making your embroidery more exciting and individual is to add an object such as a miniature spade or a tiny pot or basket. It is possible to buy these objects from shops which deal in doll's house accessories, and I am lucky enough to live near a wonderful shop which has a seemingly endless supply of tiny daffodils, apples, trowels, and so on. Of course, if you prefer, then you can make many of these extras from modelling clay. Most craft shops sell special oven-bakable or self-hardening compounds which do not need to be fired in a kiln, and these are ideal. However, the colours of some of these clays are rather restricting, so I advise you to use a white one which you can colour as you wish once you have made your object.

Garden fork with daisies
Maureen Gitting

The focal point of this garden scene is a miniature fork, which Maureen purchased at a shop specializing in doll's house accessories. The different shades of green are accented by the white fabric daisies on the right. These have fabric-covered wire stems, which were obtained from a florist's shop. The rucked piece of fabric in the foreground, the fabric leaves, and the tufted green threads add texture to the scene.

The country garden
Elsie Bolton

The delicious looking apples in this garden have been made from tiny pieces of modelling clay, which Elsie has coloured red and green. Apart from these, together with the fabric leaves and the fabric-covered wire pergola, the rest of the embroidery consists of a mass of tiny stitches, including French knots, fly stitches, straight stitches, and lazy daisy stitches. Elsie explains, 'This piece of work was lovingly and painstakingly embroidered despite the fact that I am disabled with arthritis and wear arm/hand splints. I find creative embroidery both enjoyable and therapeutic, and I hope that similarly handicapped people will be encouraged to take up this craft.'

The bonfire
Renee Grundy

The fact that Renee has difficulty in using her right arm and hand, due to an air embolism, did not prevent her from capturing beautifully this familiar autumn scene. The bonfire is constructed from real twigs with twisted pieces of organza for the flames and smoke, and the little basket on the left holds tiny pieces of kindling wood. The greenhouse consists simply of straight stitches which have been angled cleverly to give a three-dimensional effect. The trees are formed from a mixture of crocheted chains and fly stitches, whilst the autumn foliage is made up of French knots, bullion knots, and straight stitches. The subtle colours of the chiffon in the background complete the autumnal mood.

Wire and wood

With a little imagination, florists' wire, lollipop sticks, matchsticks, and wood from modelling shops can be turned into a marvellous array of fences. Trellis-work can also be woven, and twigs from the garden can be used to make pergolas and kindling for bonfires.

Wrought iron railings
Barbara Griffiths

Barbara admits that this embroidery was a joint venture, as her husband made the fence for her from florists' wire. Barbara painted the bricks with a flat-ended paintbrush, and used a mixture of straight stitches, fly stitches, French knots, and tufting to create the flowers, foliage, and window.

View of a church on a snowy day
Cecilia Henderson

This atmospheric, wintry scene has a tiny 'snow-capped' wooden fence in the foreground and a miniature road sign made from polystyrene. To create the impression of snow, Cecilia has rucked up a second piece of silk and attached it to the lower half of the embroidery. The stitches she has used include straight stitches, fly stitches, seeding stitches, French knots, and crocheted chains.

Stones

Stones can be used to give a real air of authenticity to your embroidery. The problem is, how do you attach them? There are various traditional methods of sewing stones on to fabric but, unfortunately, none appear to suit this particular type of embroidery. They all seem to look very contrived and unnatural, and even the most chaotic stitchwork looks artificial.

In my classes, we tried blanket stitch bars and strands of silk thread to look like grasses. We wove threads together to look like wire netting, but still the stones popped out. One day, May, one of my students, rang

Autumn in the Lake District
May Moores

May's landscape proves how effective little chiffon bags are for attaching real stones to an embroidery. The water consists of a piece of 'butterfly' fabric, whilst the trees in the background are made up of a variety of stitches all of which have been worked on cold-water soluble fabric.

Cottage garden at Tarnbrook
Chris Clowes

This embroidery is based upon a photograph which Chris took whilst out walking one day. It shows, very effectively, how silk stones can be used, and it also includes a gate which has been made in a similar way. The trailing fabric leaves enhance the textural, three-dimensional appearance of the wall. The stitches used for the flowers and foliage include seeding stitches, French knots, fly stitches, straight stitches, and lazy daisy stitches.

me to say that she was not going to waste any more time trying to sew the boulders into her raging river, and that instead she was going to put a still pond into the foreground. It took her twenty minutes to drive to my house, by which time I had scoured a dozen books and emptied a similar number of drawers to try to find a satisfactory way of securing stones to the river bed. In the process, some very fine chiffon material fell on to the floor beside a Dolly Varden style bag. I had found the answer! It was to make a bag from chiffon, inside which the stone could be trapped securely. This could then be attached to the embroidery easily using a few tiny stitches.

Silk stones and bricks

If you do not wish to use real stones or model bricks, then it is possible to make your own from silk. To create a brick wall, firstly you need to paint some silk the colour of the brick that you have chosen. If you want a rusty-coloured wall, then look at one and see how many different shades of rust there are in it. Try to find at least three or four shades. Using watercolour paints, splatter a variety of these shades over your piece of silk until they all blend into each other. Then, dry the silk. Cut some small bricks from mounting card and cover each one with a piece of the stained silk. Next, glue the edge of the silk to the back of the mounting card. The bricks can now be sewn down, using the smallest of stitches which just catch the corner of each one. If you wish, then you can embroider a few French knots or some seeding stitches on to the silk to add a texture. Also, try creating a tuft of moss or lichen between the bricks. If you have any silk left, then you could make some small plant pots using the same method as for the bricks.

Shutters and doors

The same principle for making silk-covered bricks and stones applies to making shutters and doors. Instead of splattering the silk with different shades of paint, you need to paint stripes on to the silk to give the impression of planks of wood. This is easier to do if you stretch your silk on to an embroidery frame first.

House in Provence
Anne Purker

To create the shutters, so characteristic of a French house, Anne painted some silk with stripes, using a flat-ended paintbrush. Then, she stretched it over two rectangles of mounting card. She made the crossbars in the same way and attached them to the shutters with French knots. The plant pots in the foreground also consist of silk-covered card, and are filled with a mixture of fabric and thread flowers. The wistaria flowers are clusters of French knots worked on cold-water soluble fabric, whilst the trunk of the plant is made up of painted pieces of silk which have been twisted together. The wall and window of the house consist of a mass of straight stitches, with long stitches for the bars of the window.

Staining a wall

Staining a wall is not as difficult as it might seem. Firstly, try it on paper and, as it is your first wall, think on a small scale. Very faintly draw the wall, or trace a picture of a wall, on to plain paper. Next, think about the colour. For example, should you choose to paint a red brick wall, then look first at a real red brick wall. The bricks are not all of the same shade – some are paler than others, and some may even have a greenish or bluish tinge to them. Try to find at least four or five shades in the wall, then put the colours on to a white plate or palette. Be as frugal as possible with the paint and use plenty of water, remembering that your aim is not to create a painting but to stain your silk so that you can embroider upon it. If the colours on the plate run into each other then do not worry, as this will give you more shades with which to work. Use a flat-ended paintbrush, if possible the same width as your bricks, and dip it into one of the patches of paint. Then, simply pick out odd bricks at random and try to paint them with one sweep of the brush. When you have used all of the paint on your brush, do not wash it but simply dip it into another shade and, again with one sweep of the brush, paint in a few more bricks. Keep working until the wall is totally covered. If it looks too clean or too pale when it dries, then erase any pencil lines that are showing and wash one of the colours from your plate straight over the entire wall. This will create the cement colour between the bricks and cover any areas that have been missed accidentally by the brush. Wait for the wall to dry. If some bricks seem to have blended too far into the background, then just paint them in again with one brush stroke.

Having learnt how to paint a brick wall on paper, now try it out on silk. Start by drawing the bricks on to another piece of paper, but this time do not draw faintly. You can even use a felt-tipped pen if you wish. Place your embroidery frame, stretched with silk only, on top of the drawing of your wall, making sure that the silk is on the top section of the frame rather than touching the paper. You should be able to see the drawing of the bricks very clearly through the fine silk. Now, apply the paint to the silk in the same way as you applied it to the paper. You might find it easier if you cover one eye. This will give you a flat impression of the wall rather than a three-dimensional view. Because the silk is absorbent, the colour will run a little. However, do not worry, as this will look like cement between the bricks. Once the silk has been stained, dry it. If it is too pale, then either wash a colour over the lot or paint each brick again. If you happen to get two colours on one brick, then even better! Conversely, if you think that the wall looks too dark, then leave the silk in the frame and put it under the tap to remove some of the paint. Dry the silk, take it off the frame, then add the cotton backing and put both fabrics back on to the ring as one. You are now ready to stitch.

Painted wall with round window
Judy Hargreaves

To create this unusual 'scene within a scene', firstly Judy worked the small embroidery seen through the round window. Then, on a new piece of silk, she painted the wall with a flat-ended paintbrush before starting to stitch. For the rambling rose on the left and the foliage in the foreground, she has used a mixture of stiffened fabrics, hessian threads, and pieces of covered florists' wire. To add to the three-dimensional effect, she has cleverly brought the foliage over the inner mount but under the top mount. The flowers in the middle distance are made up of both fabrics and threads, the stitches used including fly stitches, straight stitches, French knots, and clusters of French knots worked on cold-water soluble fabric.

Garden fork beside a wall
Maureen Gitting

To create her wall, Maureen chose to embroider each individual brick using French knots. As you can see, these give a wonderful texture, but are very time-consuming to do! The areas of concrete between the bricks are defined by a rusty-coloured stain, which Maureen applied to the whole wall before starting to stitch. The flowers and foliage consist of a mixture of bullion knots, tufting, French knots, fly stitches, straight stitches, and lazy daisy stitches. A miniature fork provides the focal point of the picture.

Church doorway
Mary Noden

This unusual doorway has been embroidered and then stretched over mounting card to give a three-dimensional effect. Each brick is made up of straight stitches, with very long stitches forming the door. The path in the foreground consists of a mass of tiny seeding stitches, whilst the garland of flowers over the door has been worked using a variety of stitches on cold-water soluble fabric. The gold shape at the top of the sundial has been made from one of Mary's tooth fillings, so, literally, a part of her is in this embroidery!

Embroidering a wall

The next stage on from staining a wall is to embroider one. If you find it a problem imagining where the bricks are to be placed, then trace or draw some on to your silk. Make sure that you cover these guidelines with threads once you start to embroider. The choice of stitches is entirely up to you, but the embroideries illustrated in this section should give you some ideas. An interesting possibility is to stain the wall first, not defining individual bricks but simply brushing a pale rust wash over the entire area to be embroidered. You can then leave some areas of the brick without stitches to create a textural effect.

Foxgloves in front of a window
Marie Bell

In this embroidery, Marie has cunningly disguised the fact that she has not embroidered a single brick! Having decided that she did not want to paint or embroider individual bricks, she painted the whole background a mixture of black and dark green. Then, she covered the wall with lazy daisy stitches, using straight stitches for the window frame and glazing bars. The flowers and foliage are made up of lazy daisy stitches, straight stitches, French knots, fly stitches, and rings of blanket stitches for the small pink roses on the right. A few fabric leaves add extra textural interest to the scene.

Creating depth and distance

If you wish to create the impression of depth and distance in your landscapes, then you need to know a little about using tone and perspective. In this section, I describe some simple ways of achieving both. Remember, too, to refer to the section on 'just looking' (see pages 8–15), as this also contains useful information on how tone and perspective work.

Using tone

Tone is not difficult to use. Just remember that the further away, for example, a mountain is, the smaller, paler, and more grey it will appear. The nearer a mountain is, the larger and more colourful it will be. On the following pages you can see four examples of how tone can be used to create a feeling of depth.

Sunset in the Canadian Rockies
Carole Charlesworth

This embroidery was inspired by a photograph which Carole took whilst on holiday in the Canadian Rockies. It shows, very simply, how tone can be used to create a feeling of depth and distance. Firstly, Carole stained the sky a pale blue colour. Then, for the mountains, she cut two pieces of silk, one paler than the other, and placed them on to the background silk. To hold the mountains in place, she worked the foreground, using a mixture of straight and fly stitches for the conifers, and stained and stiffened fabric for the cranberries.

The elephant
Irene Scott

Having embroidered a number of gardens, Irene was looking for something different to do when she came across this picture in a travel brochure. She added the tree herself, to give greater interest to the scene. To give the impression of the distant mountain, Irene painted it on to a separate piece of silk, then cut it out and trapped it between the background silk and the cotton sheeting. She used a series of overlapping layers of chiffon to create the colours of the middle distance and the foreground. The tree is worked in a mixture of French knots and crocheted chains, whilst the surrounding foliage includes fly stitches, lazy daisy stitches, and straight stitches. The elephant is made of a variety of grey straight stitches, with tusks of oven-bakable modelling clay.

Harvest time
Joyce Topliss

*Tone has been used to very dramatic effect in this moody scene, which was inspired by a
picture in a book on the countryside. Layers of darkly coloured chiffon form the sky,
over which have been embroidered the trees in a mixture of fly stitches and dark green
French knots. To create the field of corn, Joyce worked the whole area in straight stitch,
then cut and fluffed up about one-third of the stitches, before working yet more on top of
them. The sheaves of corn are formed simply from short lengths of thread which have
been tied together in the middle.*

Japanese waterfall in autumn
Gillian Nuttall

With a range of carefully chosen coloured threads, Gillian has made very subtle use of tone in order to create the feeling of depth in this embroidery. The stitches she has used include lazy daisy stitches and French knots for the foliage in the background, straight stitches in the middle distance behind the waterfall, and a mixture of French knots, straight stitches, and lazy daisy stitches worked on cold-water soluble fabric for the foreground. A mass of fabric leaves, stained a lovely autumnal colour, have been used to add extra three-dimensional interest. The waterfall itself is made from a piece of plaited, silky nylon thread, which Gillian has simply unravelled.

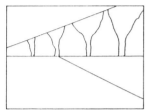

Using perspective

I have decided not to try to explain perspective in this book. It is a very difficult and technical way of describing distance, and I think that it is better just to show you a simple way of achieving it in your embroideries.

Hold a piece of clear glass up to your eye and look through it at the view that you wish to interpret, making sure that the whole view can be seen within the confines of the glass. Then, close one eye and simply trace on to the glass, with a felt-tipped pen, what you can see. Place the glass on to a sheet of white paper and, hey presto, your design should be clear enough for you to transfer on to your silk.

For each of the embroideries illustrated in this section, I have drawn a very simple plan to show how perspective has been used. If you wish to explore the subject in greater depth, then I am sure that your local library will be able to help you.

Solomon's Temple
Janice Walker

This tiny embroidery was inspired by a country walk. Janice explains, 'After a tour of the cold, damp Poole's Cavern, it was lovely to walk through Grin Low Woods and up the hill to Solomon's Temple to view the surrounding countryside. I took many photographs, upon which I based this picture, in an attempt to capture some of the magic of that afternoon.' In order to give the feeling of distance and of looking up a hill, Janice has kept the flowers in the foreground deliberately low. The stitches she has used include seeding stitches, French knots, straight stitches, tufting, and fly stitches.

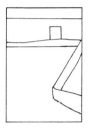

The tunnel
Christine Flegg

Looking at this realistic embroidery, it is difficult not to wonder what is on the other side of the tunnel! Firstly, Christine painted the wall, then she worked seeding stitches to create the shape of the tunnel entrance, and long, black straight stitches to give the impression of the tunnel receding into the distance. A mass of green crocheted chains form the ivy growing over the top of the tunnel, whilst the foreground foliage is made up of fly stitches, lazy daisy stitches, French knots, and straight stitches.

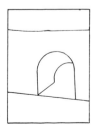

Anne Hathaway's cottage
Dorothy Farnell
Loaned by kind permission of the late Mrs Farnell's daughter, Sue Tait.

This delicate and rather complex embroidery is based upon a photograph which Dorothy saw in a calendar. It makes full use of perspective and includes a whole range of stitches – French knots, fly stitches, straight stitches, seeding stitches, and blanket stitches. It also contains a few fabric flowers and leaves in the foreground.

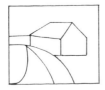

Poppy field
Leila Sutcliffe

This scene demonstrates beautifully how tone and perspective can be used together to create the impression of depth and distance. The grass pales in colour as it recedes into the distance, and the poppies change from pieces of stained fabric in the foreground to French knots in the middle distance and tiny seeding stitches in the far distance. The trees consist of fly stitches and French knots, and the pale, distant hill is a piece of fabric which has been trapped between the silk and the cotton backing fabric. To increase the feeling of depth, Leila has also made use of the mount by adding a few painted and tissue paper poppies to the bottom right-hand corner.

61

Embroidering an outer mount

An embroidered outer mount can add considerable interest to a land-scape. It can be either a continuation of the embroidery or a separate thought altogether – both look good.

In the embroidery illustrated here, Barbara decided to continue her theme on to her mount. Firstly, she traced the original central embroidery so that she could link up the path and the herbaceous border. Then, she cut the tracing out and placed it on to another piece of silk which she had stretched already on a larger frame. With an air-soluble pen, she marked where the path was to begin. She was then able to embroider the mount, secure in the knowledge that it would match up exactly with the original embroidery. It was her choice to make the mount 3.75 cm (1½in) wide – it could just as easily have been 6mm (¼in) or 15cm (6in) wide!

If you choose to make an embroidered mount, then once you have completed the embroidery you have to stretch the silk over card. To do this, firstly cut out the silk, leaving between 1.25–2.5 cm (½-1in) of spare fabric around both the outer and the inner edges of the embroidery. Then, place the embroidery on to a piece of mounting card and, using a pin, prick all the way around the edges of the stitching. Remove the embroidery to reveal the pricked shape clearly marked on the mounting card. Now, join the pricked marks with a pencil and, with a craft knife, carefully cut out the shape. Place the embroidery face down on to a table, position the card on top of it, and glue the spare fabric to the back of the card. Whilst the glue is still slightly damp, turn the mount over and check that the silk is not cockled and that the grain looks straight.

The inner embroidery, with a stained brick wall, French knot path, and flower border of assorted stitches.

The embroidered mount, again with a stained brick wall, French knot path, and flower border of assorted stitches. The plant pots consist of stained silk stretched over mounting card, with stiffened threads in one and fabric flowers in the other.

Round garden
Barbara Sherlock

*The complete scene, made up of the inner embroidery, the embroidered mount, and
two further mounts of pink card.*

Index